Y0-DYI-154

New Hanover County Public Library

A Home
for Me

Homes ABC

Lola M. Schaefer

Heinemann Library
Chicago, Illinois

©2003 Reed Educational & Professional Publishing
Published by Heinemann Library,
an imprint of Reed Educational & Professional Publishing
Chicago, IL

Customer Service 888-454-2279
Visit our website at www.heinemannlibrary.com

Designed by Sue Emerson, Heinemann Library
Printed and bound in the United States by Lake Book Manufacturing, Inc.

07 06 05 04 03
10 9 8 7 6 5 4 3 2 1

Library of Congress Cataloging-in-Publication Data
Lola M. Schaefer
    Homes ABC / Lola M. Schaefer.
        p. cm. — (A Home for Me)
Includes index.
Summary: An alphabet book which features words about different kinds of houses and homes, rooms, and people associated with them, such as the janitor who keeps an apartment building clean and safe.
    ISBN: 1-4034-0260-4 (HC), 1-4034-0483-6 (Pbk.)
    1. Dwellings—Juvenile literature. 2. Rooms—Juvenile literature. [1. Dwellings. 2. Alphabet.] I. Title. II. Series: Schaefer, Lola M., 1950–.
    GT172.S34 2002
    307.3'36—dc21

                        2001008143

Acknowledgments
The author and publishers are grateful to the following for permission to reproduce copyright material:
pp. 3, 4, 6, 16, 17 Robert Lifson/Heinemann Library; pp. 5L, 14 George Payne/www.cajunimages.com; pp. 5R, 10, 12, 13, 20 Greg Williams/Heinemann Library; p. 7 Karen Bussolini; p. 8 B & C Alexander; p. 9 Michael Malyszko/FPG International/Getty Images; p. 11 Courtesy of Houseboat Magazine; p. 15 Charles Cook; p. 18 Douglas Keister; p. 19 Jill Birschbach/Heinemann Library; p. 21 Mark E. Gibson/Visuals Unlimited; p. 22 David June; p. 23 (row 1, L-R) David June, Karen Bussolini, Greg Williams/Heinemann Library, Heinemann Library; p. 23 (row 2, L-R) Jill Birschbach/Heinemann Library, B & C Alexander, DWPL/Visuals Unlimited, Douglas Keister; p. 23 (row 3, L-R) Greg Williams/Heinemann Library, Michael Malyszko/FPG International/Getty Images, Charles Cook, Douglas Keister; p. 23 (row 4) Robert Lifson/Heinemann Library; back cover (L-R) Karen Bussolini, B & C Alexander

Photo research by Amor Montes de Oca
Cover photographs (clockwise from TL) B & C Alexander, Courtesy of Houseboat Magazine, Mark E. Gibson/Corbis

Every effort has been made to contact copyright holders of any material reproduced in this book. Any omissions will be rectified in subsequent printings if notice is given to the publisher.

Special thanks to our advisory panel for their help in the preparation of this book:

Eileen Day, Preschool teacher
Chicago, IL

Ellen Dolmetsch,
Library Media Specialist
Wilmington, DE

Kathleen Gilbert,
Second Grade Teacher
Round Rock, TX

Sandra Gilbert,
Library Media Specialist
Houston, TX

Angela Leeper,
Educational Consultant
North Carolina Department
of Public Instruction
Raleigh, NC

Pam McDonald,
Reading Support Specialist
Winter Springs, FL

Melinda Murphy,
Library Media Specialist
Houston, TX

Some words are shown in bold, **like this.**
You can find them in the picture glossary on page 23.

A a Apartment

A family of four lives in this apartment.

This is their home.

B b Bathroom
C c Closet

People take baths in a bathroom.

Many bathrooms have a closet.

D d Door
E e Elevator

Some **apartment buildings** have big front doors.

There are **elevators** to take people up or down.

F f   Fireplace

Some homes have a **fireplace**.

G g   Greenhouse

greenhouse

Some homes have a **greenhouse.**

Plants can grow in a greenhouse all year.

H h House
I i Igloo

An **igloo** is a kind of house.

Igloos are made of ice
and snow.

Jj   Janitor

Many **apartment buildings**
have **janitors**.

Janitors keep the building
clean and safe.

K k   Kitchen

People cook food in a kitchen.

This kitchen is in a mobile home.

Ll Laundry Room

A laundry room is a place for people to wash their clothes.

This laundry room is on a houseboat.

M m Mobile Home

Most mobile homes are shaped like **rectangles**.

N n Nursery

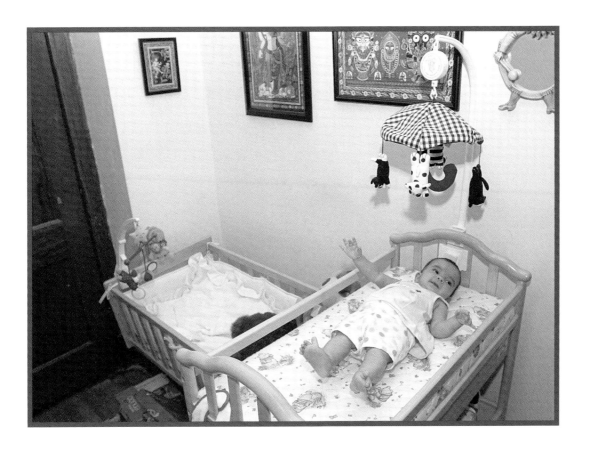

Some homes have a room for a baby.

This room is called a **nursery**.

O o   Outside
P p   Patio

Families sit outside on their **patios**.

Q q Queen-sized Bed

Queen-sized beds are large.

Two people can sleep side by side.

R r   Refrigerator

There is a refrigerator in this kitchen.

Refrigerators keep food cold and fresh.

S s   Stairs

People walk up and down stairs in their homes.

Tt Trailer

Mobile homes are sometimes called **trailers.**

That is because they can be pulled behind a big truck.

U u   Underground

Some houses and apartments have **basements.**

A basement is a big room underground.

V v View
W w Window

What you see from your home is called a view.

This window has a view of the city.

X x   Exercise
Y y   Yard

Most houses have a **yard**.

Playing in the yard is good exercise.

Zz   Zzzzz

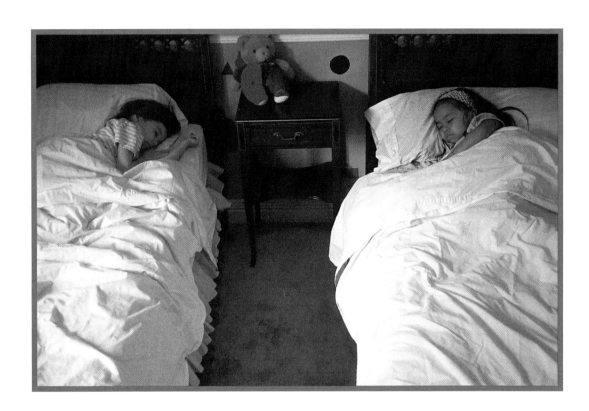

At the end of the day, most people sleep in their own beds at home.

Zzzzz . . .

Picture Glossary

apartment building
pages 5, 9

greenhouse
page 7

nursery
page 13

rectangle
page 12

basement
page 19

igloo
page 8

patio
page 14

trailer
page 18

elevator
page 5

janitor
page 9

queen-sized bed
page 15

yard
page 21

fireplace
page 6

23

Note to Parents and Teachers

Using this book, children can practice alphabetic skills while learning interesting facts about different types of homes. Together, read *Homes ABC*. Say the names of the letters aloud, then say the target word, exaggerating the beginning of the word. For example, "/r/: Rrrr-efrigerator." Can the child think of any other words that begin with the /r/ sound? (Although the letter x is not at the beginning of the word "exercise," the /ks/ sound of the letter x is still prominent.) Try to sing the "ABC song," substituting the *Homes ABC* alphabet words for the letters a, b, c, and so on.

Index